Econo-Graphics

Budgeting
IN INFOGRAPHICS

Christina Hill

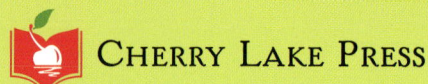

Published in the United States of America by Cherry Lake Publishing Group
Ann Arbor, Michigan
www.cherrylakepublishing.com

Reading Adviser: Beth Walker Gambro, MS, Ed., Reading Consultant, Yorkville, IL

Photo Credits: Page 1: ©Marta Shershen/Getty Images; Page 8: ©Visual Generation Inc./Getty Images; Page 14: ©Tetiana Lazunova/Getty Images; Page 16: ©Qvasimodo/Getty Images; Page 19: ©Valeriia Soloveva/Getty Images; Page 20: ©franckreporter/Getty Images; Page 21: ©Jaen Zevallos/Pixabay; Page 21: ©REDQUASAR/Pixabay; Page 21: ©Clker-Free-Vector-Images/Pixabay; Page 21: ©Clker-Free-Vector-Images/Pixabay; Page 21: ©Harisankar Sahoo/Pixabay; Page 21: ©sumit kumar/Pixabay; Page 21: ©Mohamed Hassan/Pixabay; Page 24: ©nadia_bormotova/Getty Images; Page 25: ©Varijanta/Getty Images

Copyright © 2023 by Cherry Lake Publishing Group

All rights reserved. No part of this book may be reproduced or utilized in any form or by any means without written permission from the publisher.

Cherry Lake Press is an imprint of Cherry Lake Publishing Group.

Library of Congress Cataloging-in-Publication Data
Names: Hill, Christina, author.
Title: Budgeting in infographics / Christina Hill.
Description: Ann Arbor, Michigan : Cherry Lake Press, [2023] | Series: Econo-graphics | Includes bibliographical references and index. | Audience: Ages 9-13 | Audience: Grades 4-6 | Summary: "Understanding how to wisely budget money is an important part of everyday life. In this book, readers will learn the most important financial literacy rule: Spend less than you earn. Learning about wants vs. needs will help readers make choices on how to spend, save, and invest money, especially during pandemic times. Colorful and clear graphics, such as maps, charts, and infographics, give readers an alternative to text-heavy sources. Action-based activities will leave students with real-life ideas on how to balance a budget. This book also includes a glossary, index, suggested reading and websites, and a bibliography"-- Provided by publisher.
Identifiers: LCCN 2022016901 (print) | LCCN 2022016902 (ebook) | ISBN 9781668909980 (hardcover) | ISBN 9781668911587 (paperback) | ISBN 9781668914762 (pdf)
Subjects: LCSH: Budget--Juvenile literature. | Budgets, Personal--Juvenile literature. | Finance, Public--Juvenile literature. | Finance, Personal--Juvenile literature.
Classification: LCC HJ2005 .H55 2023 (print) | LCC HJ2005 (ebook) | DDC 352.4/8--dc23/eng/20220413
LC record available at https://lccn.loc.gov/2022016901
LC ebook record available at https://lccn.loc.gov/2022016902

Cherry Lake Publishing Group would like to acknowledge the work of the Partnership for 21st Century Learning, a Network of Battelle for Kids. Please visit *http://www.battelleforkids.org/networks/p21* for more information.

Printed in the United States of America

Before embracing a career as an author, **Christina Hill** received a bachelor's degree in English from the University of California, Irvine, and a graduate degree in literature from California State University, Long Beach. When she is not writing about various subjects from sports to economics, Christina can be found hiking, mastering yoga handstands, or curled up with a classic novel. Christina lives in sunny Southern California with her husband, two sons, and beloved dog, Pepper Riley.

CONTENTS

Introduction
What Is a Budget? | 4

Chapter 1
Income and Expenses | 6

Chapter 2
Federal and State Budgets | 10

Chapter 3
Wants vs. Needs | 18

Chapter 4
Building a Budget | 22

Activity | 30
Learn More | 31
Glossary | 32
Index | 32

INTRODUCTION

What Is a Budget?

A **budget** is an economic plan for how to get money and what to spend it on. Governments, businesses, and individuals all need to create a budget. A good budget ensures that there is enough money to pay for things now and in the future.

The goal of a budget is to balance **income** and **expenses**. Income is money that is earned through **wages**, allowances, investments, and gifts. Expenses are things that the money is spent on. They may be *needed* items, such as food, clothing, and housing, or *wanted* items, such as toys and entertainment.

A Balanced Budget

Expenses:
- $5 discount movie ticket
- $2 sports drink at the Snack Shack
- $5 baseball
- $23 savings

Income:
- $10 weekly allowance
- $10 birthday-card money
- $10 for walking the neighbor's dog
- $5 for washing Grandpa's car

CHAPTER 1

Income and Expenses

To budget money, there first needs to be a source of income. Children can get allowances or gifts. Employees get paid wages.

Businesses also need money, or profit, to continue making goods or providing services. Many companies take out **loans** from the bank to get started. They also can sell shares of their company to raise money.

State and federal governments get money from **taxes**. This income helps them build roads, public schools, and provide other services.

Average Hourly Wage in the United States (1980-2020)

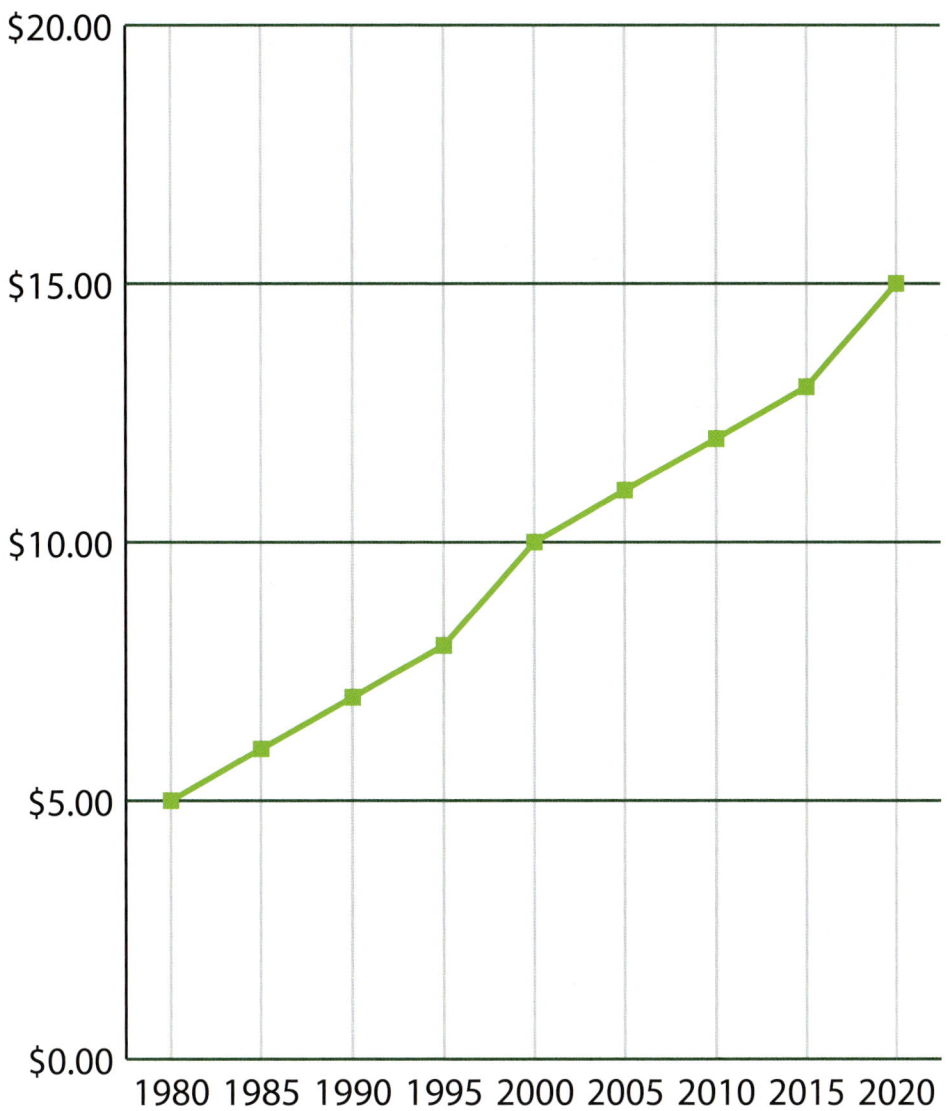

2021, Statista

Fast Facts

- Most Americans spend their money on housing, transportation, and food.
- According to the U.S. Bureau of Labor Statistics, the average American spends $1,674 on housing, $813 on transportation, and $372 on groceries in one month.

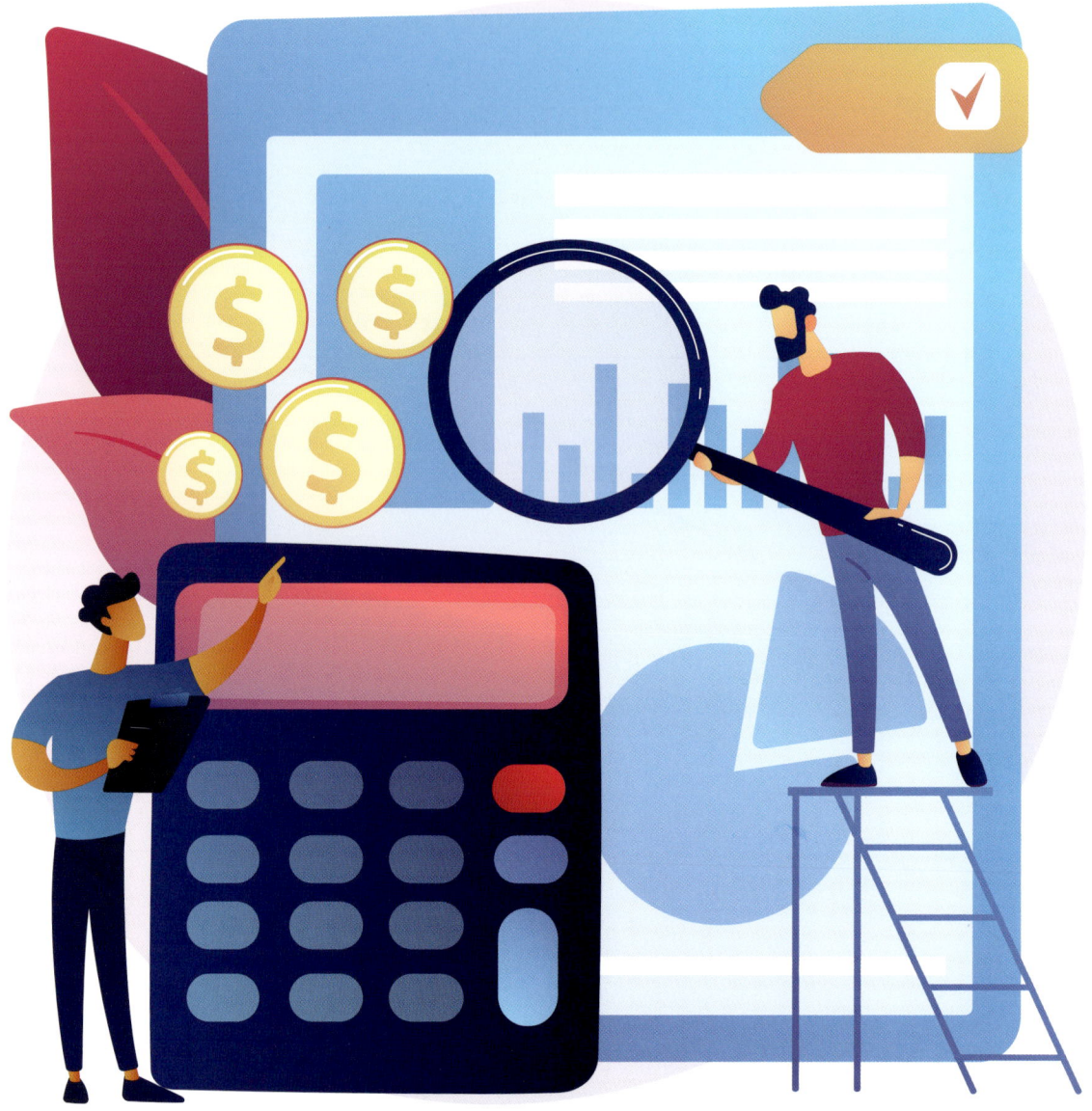

How Americans Spend Their Money

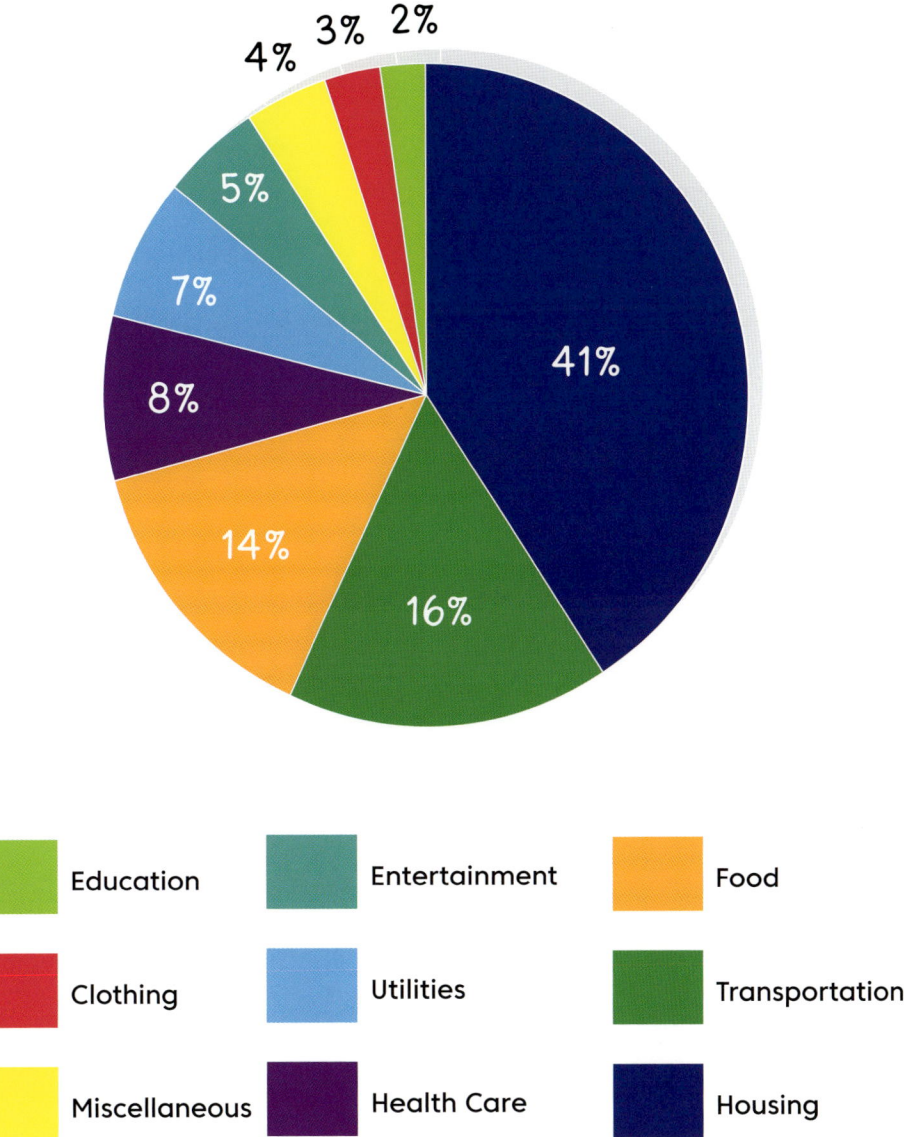

2017, U.S. Bureau of Labor Statistics

CHAPTER 2

Federal and State Budgets

In the United States, the president creates a federal budget after reviewing the budget plans from all government agencies. The president submits the budget to Congress. The House and the Senate discuss and vote on bills that show how the money will be given out. After everyone agrees, the president signs the budget into law.

The government gets most of its income from taxes. There are taxes on what citizens earn, buy, and own. The federal government collected $3.5 trillion in **revenue** in 2020. This is equal to around $10,457 per person.

What Does $3.5 Trillion Look Like?

One hundred $100 bills are equal to $10,000. This bundle could fit easily in your hand.

Take that bundle and make it worth $1 million (100 of the $10,000 bundles). This would be a much larger stack of bills.

Here is $1 billion. This is way more than you could carry around!

One trillion is 1,000 *billions*! The money would now take up a huge amount of space.

Finally, multiply the previous amount by 3.5. That's how much money the U.S. federal government collected in 2020: $3.5 trillion!

Where the U.S. Federal Government Gets Money

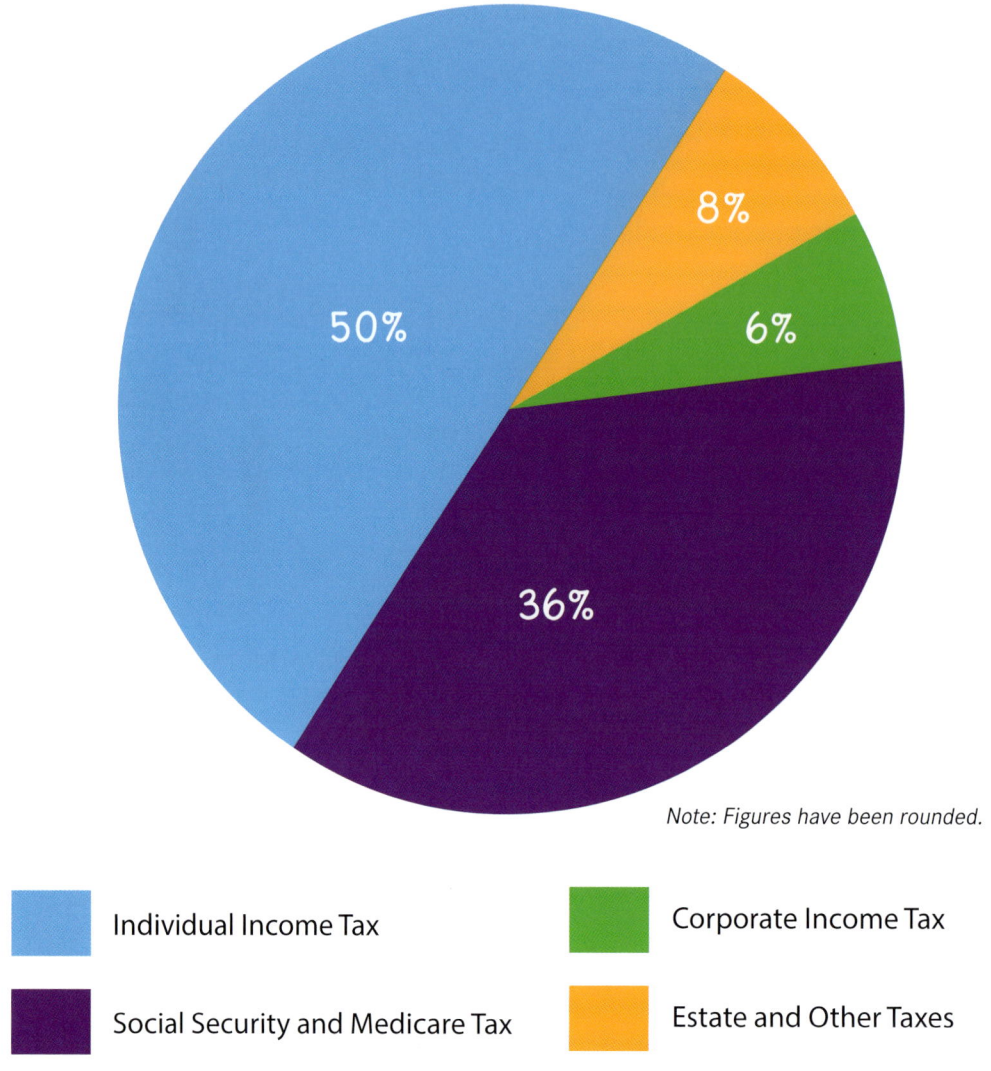

Note: Figures have been rounded.

- Individual Income Tax
- Social Security and Medicare Tax
- Corporate Income Tax
- Estate and Other Taxes

2019, Center on Budget and Policy Priorities

What the U.S. Federal Government Spends Money On

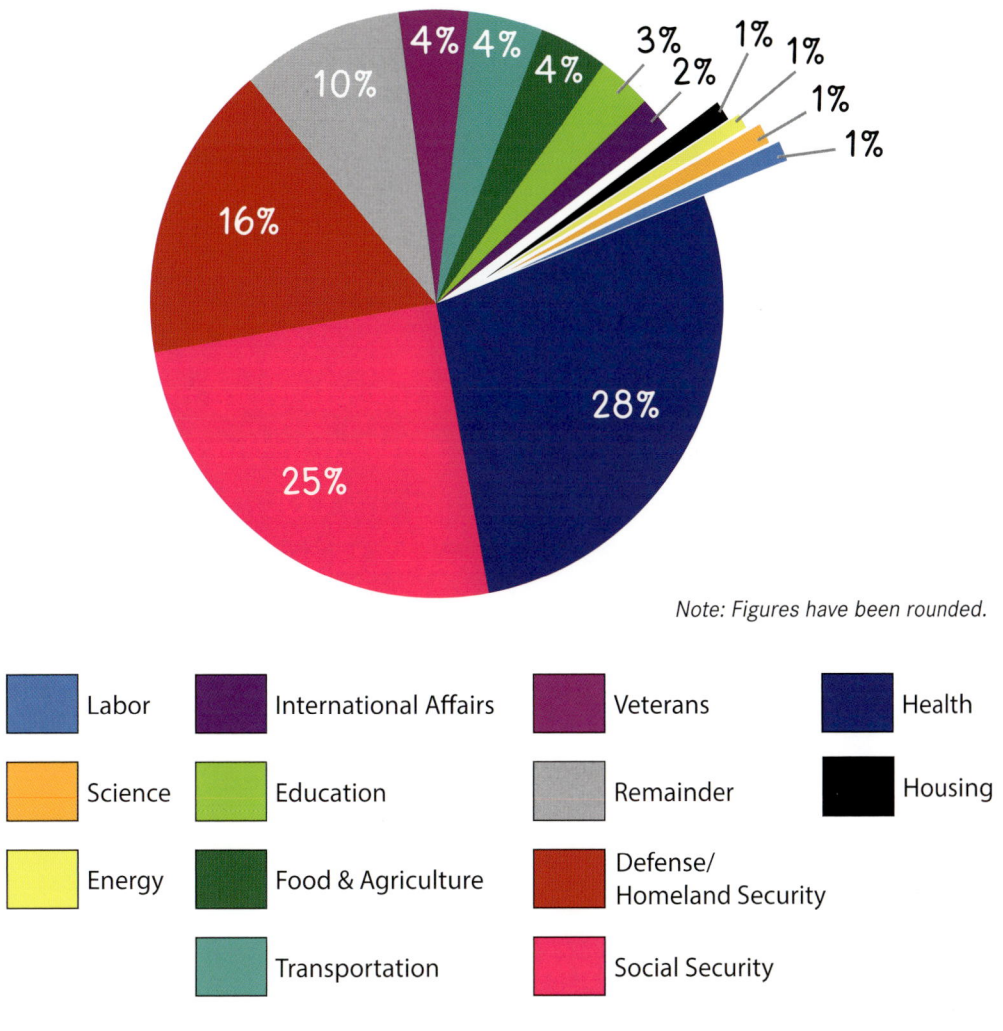

Note: Figures have been rounded.

2015, Poynter Institute

Surplus or Deficit?

A **surplus** is when the government collects more money than it spends. The last U.S. surplus was in 2001.

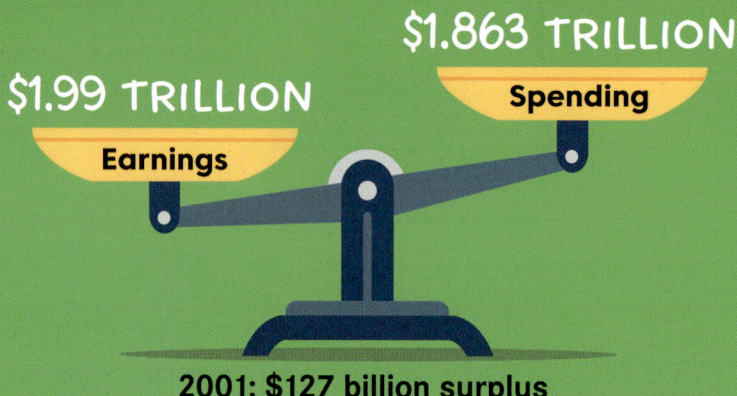

2001: $127 billion surplus

A **deficit** is when the government spends more money than it collects. There has been a deficit in the United States for 20 years. In 2020, during the COVID-19 pandemic, the federal deficit was $3.13 trillion.

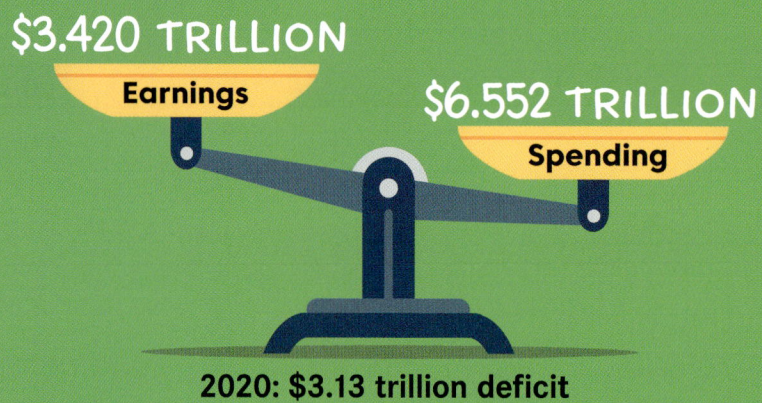

2020: $3.13 trillion deficit

2001, 2020, U.S. Federal Budget

The U.S. Federal Deficit (2001–2021)

The graph shows a spike in 2020 due to the COVID-19 pandemic. The federal government spent more money on stimulus checks for individuals and businesses to help them recover from job loss and poor sales.

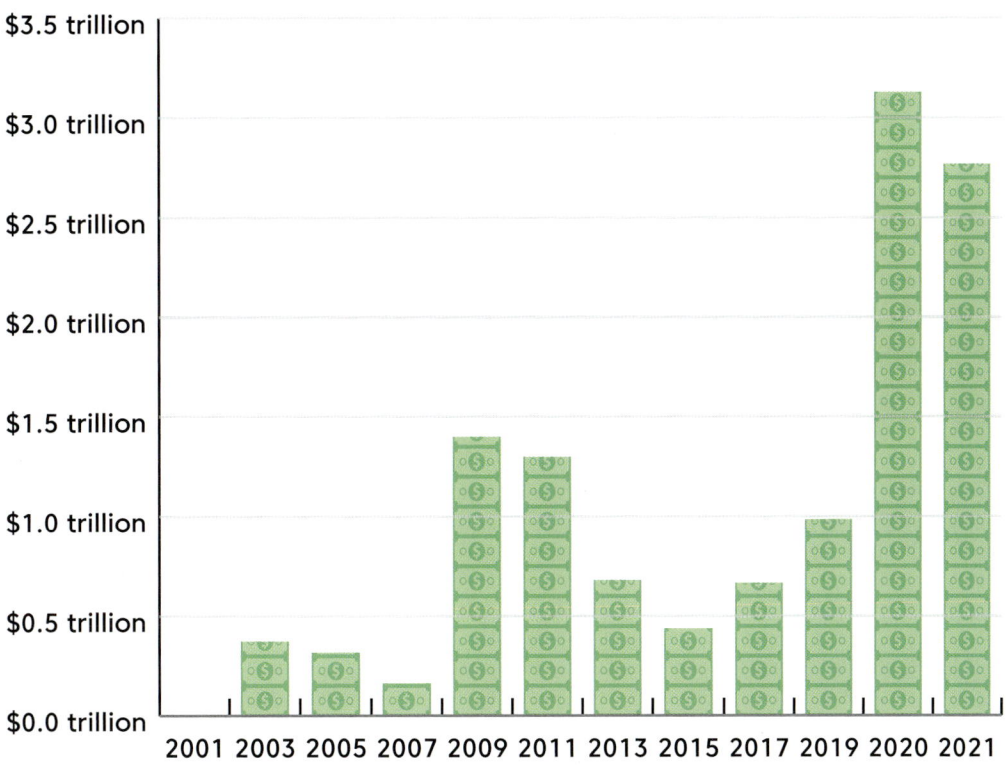

2021, Monthly Treasury Statement

Rainy Day Fund

All states have a budget, just like the federal government. They also have a rainy day fund, which is a savings account where surplus money is set aside. This money is used in times of emergency or deficit.

Rainy Day Funds by U.S. State

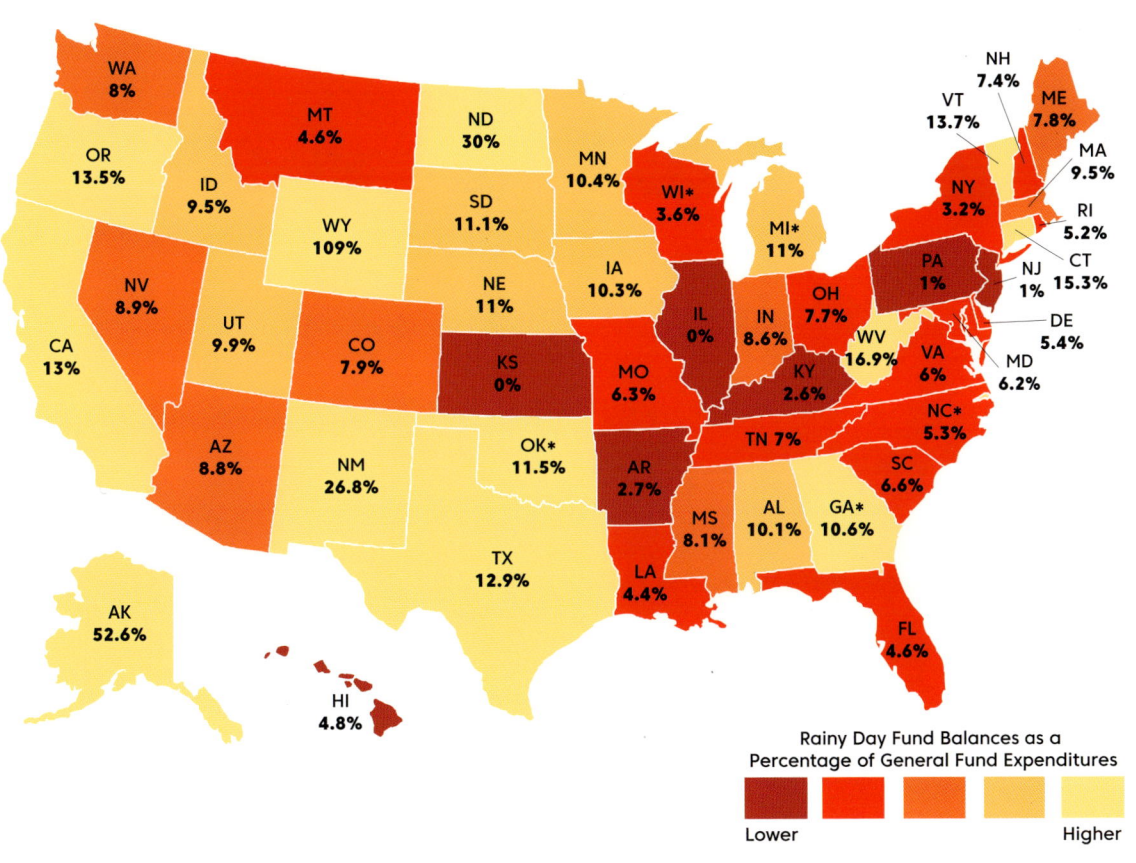

*Note: D.C. is not included in the source material. The figure for Georgia is from 2018. Figures for MI, NC, OK, and WI are from 2019. All other figures are for 2020.

2019, National Association of State Budget Offices

CHAPTER 3

Wants vs. Needs

An ideal budget must be a balance between income, spending, and savings. Wants and needs must be considered. Needs come first, and wants come second. Food, clothing, utilities, and housing are called needs because they are important for survival.

Governments, businesses, and individuals also have things they want to spend money on. These things may include a new government program, new office chairs, a vacation, the latest video game, or movie tickets. All of these things are wants because they are not needed for survival.

Wants vs. Needs

Things that are desired but not essential for survival	vs.	Essential for survival
Changes over time	vs.	Does not change
Different for all people	vs.	Same for all people

Tracking your monthly expenses is a good way to clearly see where your money is going.

When creating a budget, 50 percent of one's income should be set aside for needs. What takes the other half of the budget pie? A smart choice is to set aside 20 percent for savings and investments for the future. That leaves 30 percent for wants.

Dividing the Budget Pie

21

CHAPTER 4

Building a Budget

The ultimate goal is to have a *balanced* budget, where needs, wants, and savings are accounted for. **Debt** occurs when expenses outweigh income and savings.

Budgets are unique to each individual, family, state, and government. Not everyone has the same wants. Income can change based on bonuses, raises, or job promotions or losses. Creating a budget is a balancing act that needs to be adjusted as income and expenses change.

Cost of Living by U.S. State

The cost of living varies because prices for housing, food, and health care are more expensive in some states. Below, the cost of living is represented by the number 100.

Most Expensive State

This means it costs 96.3% MORE to live in Hawaii than in any other state. The average home price in Hawaii is more than $1 million. Groceries are more expensive because food is shipped to the islands from the mainland.

HAWAII
196.3

MISSISSIPPI
84.8

Least Expensive State

This means it is 15.2% cheaper to live in Mississippi. House prices are lower here than in any other state, with the average home price at about $150,000.

Right in the Middle

At 100.7, Virginia is almost exactly at the average cost of living. While home prices are slightly higher than average, transportation and groceries are lower, which balances out.

VIRGINIA
100.7

2021, World Population Review

The number one rule in building a balanced budget:

Spend LESS than you earn!

Calculating Debt-to-Income Ratio

Monthly debt (housing, car payments, credit cards, bills) divided by monthly income equals a debt-to-income (DTI) ratio.

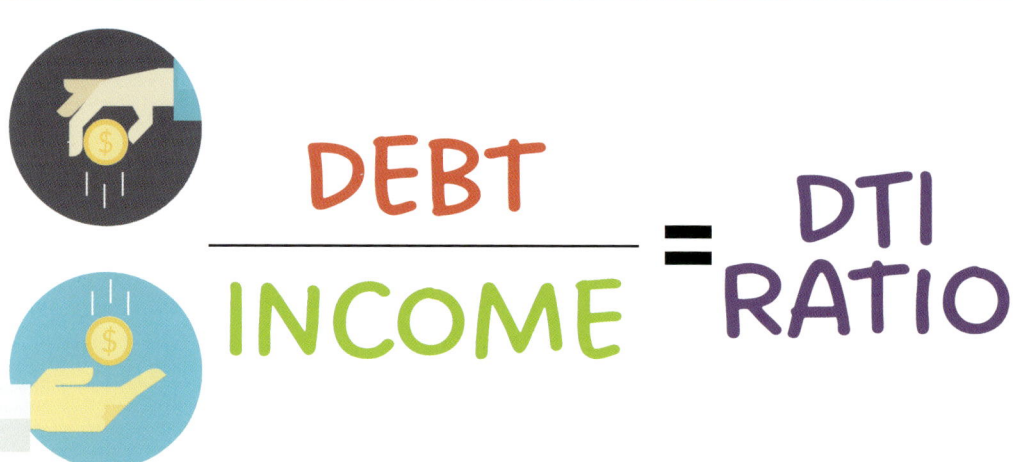

Debt-to-Income Ratio Ranges

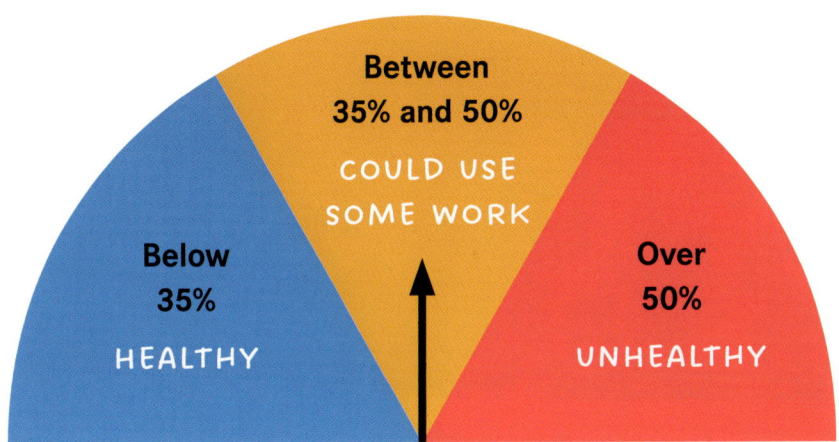

Quiz Time!

Vidar pays $1,000 a month for his house. He pays $100 for his car and $400 for the rest of his monthly bills. He makes $5,000 a month in income. Is his debt-to-income ratio healthy?

Answer: Yes; Vidar's monthly debt ($1,500) divided by his monthly income ($5,000) equals a DTI ratio of 30%. Below 35% is considered healthy.

Average Credit Card Debt by U.S. State (2021)

The average American has $5,525 in credit card debt.

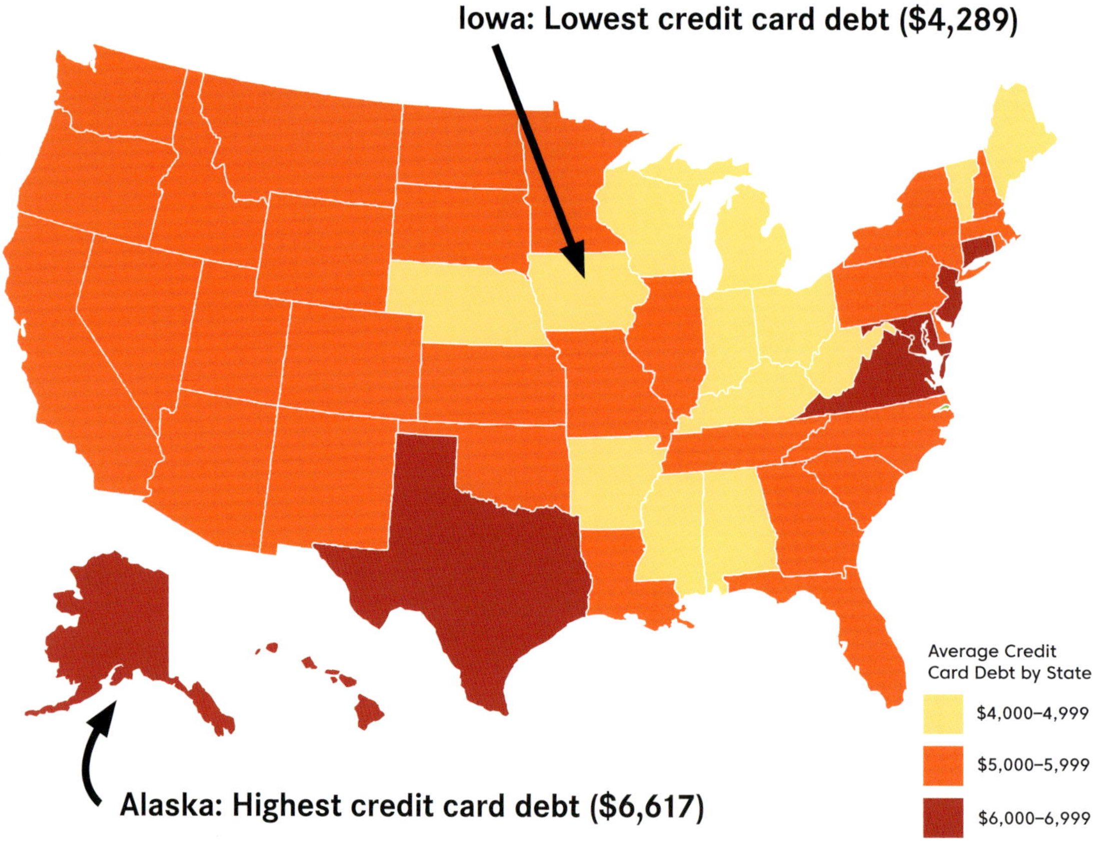

Iowa: Lowest credit card debt ($4,289)

Alaska: Highest credit card debt ($6,617)

Average Credit Card Debt by State
- $4,000–4,999
- $5,000–5,999
- $6,000–6,999

2021, Experian

How Much Have You Saved?

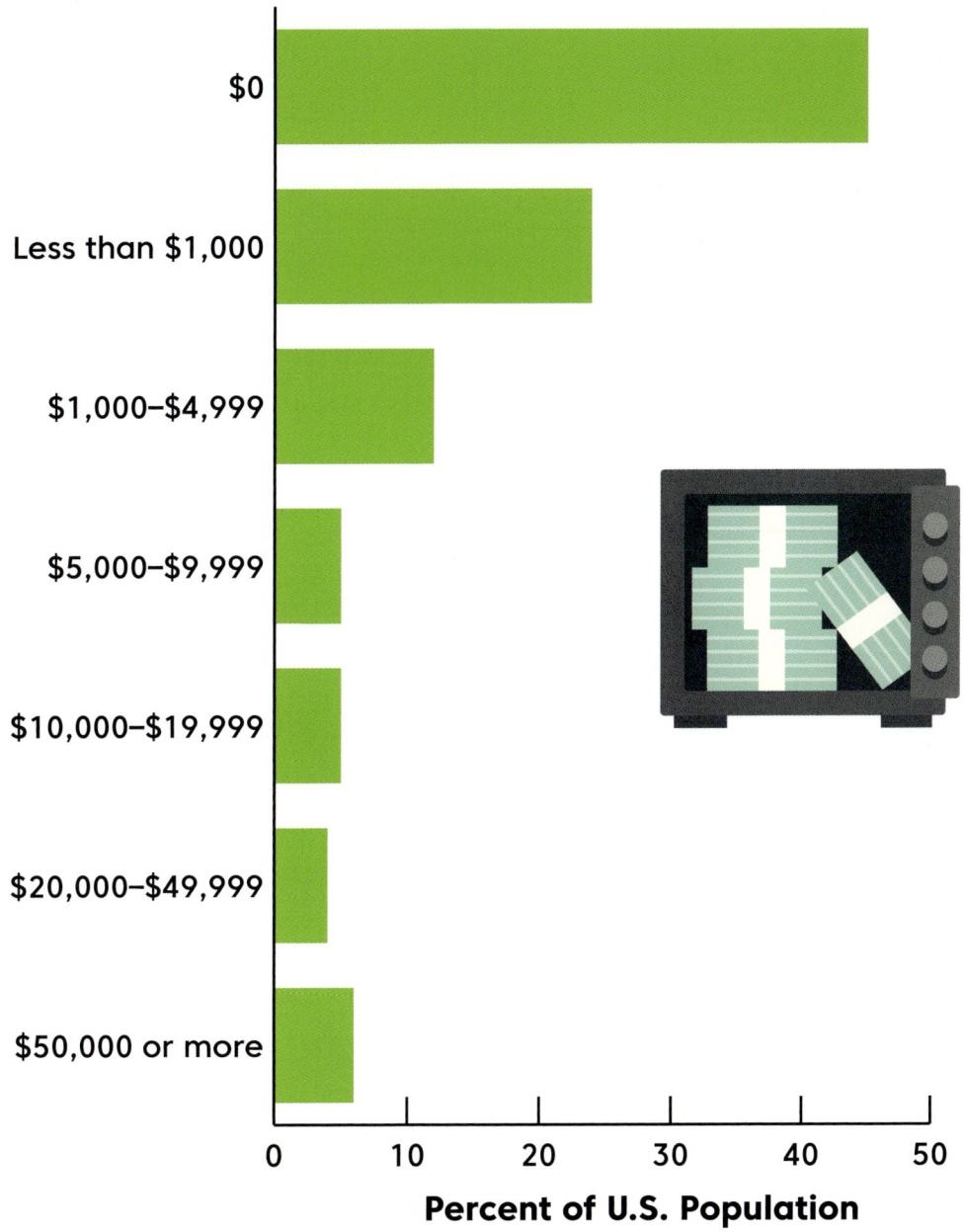

2019, GOBankingRates

How to Build a Budget

Set a Budget Goal

How much money are you trying to save by the end of each month?

List Your Income

How much money do you gain each month through wages, gifts, allowances, or investments?

List Your Expenses

Note that this amount may change each month as prices go up and down.

Set Aside Savings

Remember your budget goal when setting aside your savings.

Track Everything

A dollar here or there will add up quickly! Continue to subtract every expense from your earnings.

Adjust

Continue to adjust the budget as needed to meet your goals.

Activity

Create a Balanced Budget

Your big sister just got her first job delivering pizza. She knows you are a financial expert and wants your help to make a budget. Her goal is to save $300 per month for six months. Her monthly income is $1,200. Her monthly expenses include her car payment of $200. She also spends $100 a month on gas and $300 on food and clothing.

Here are a few things to keep in mind:

- In August, your family is taking a vacation to the beach. Your sister wants to budget $50 for souvenirs and $300 for a new surfboard.
- In September, she wants to go to a concert. The ticket costs $50.
- Your sister's birthday is in November, and your grandma always sends her $100.

Create a chart to help your sister track her money. How much will she have left over at the end of the year? How much money would you recommend she start saving each month to build a healthy savings account?

MONTH	DESCRIPTION	INCOME	EXPENSES	BALANCE
July				
August				
September				
October				
November				
December				

Learn More

Books

Dakers, Diane. *The Bottom Line: Money Basics*. New York, NY: Crabtree Publishing, 2017.

Minden, Cecilia. *Living on a Budget*. New York, NY: Smartbook Media Inc., 2017.

Websites

Britannica Kids: Budget
https://kids.britannica.com/students/article/budget/273391

The Mint: Fun for Kids
https://www.themint.org/kids

Bibliography

Chatzky, Jean. "Five Things You Need to Know About Money." April 29, 2021. https://www.timeforkids.com/partner/pwc/g4/five-things-you-need-to-know-about-money

Lockert, Melanie. "What Is Economic Surplus and How Does It Work?" October 21, 2021. https://www.businessinsider.com/surplus-definition

O'Shea, Bev, and Lauren Schwahn. "Budgeting 101: How to Budget Money." December 17, 2021. https://www.nerdwallet.com/article/finance/how-to-budget

Vohwinkle, Jeremy. "How to Make a Personal Budget in 6 Easy Steps." Last modified January 11, 2022. https://www.thebalance.com/how-to-make-a-budget-1289587

Glossary

budget (BUHJ-it) an amount of money available for spending that is based on a plan for how it will be spent

debt (DET) an amount of money that you owe to a person, bank, or company

deficit (DEF-uh-sit) an amount of money that is less than the amount that is needed

expenses (ik-SPENS-ez) the amounts of money that are needed to pay for and buy things

income (IN-kuhm) money received for work or through investments on a regular basis

loans (LOHNZ) amounts of money that are given to someone with a promise that they will be paid back

revenue (REV-uh-noo) money that is made by or paid to a business or an organization

surplus (SUR-pluhs) an amount that is more than the amount needed

taxes (TAKS-ez) an amount of money that a government requires citizens to pay that is used to fund the things the government provides for them

wages (WAYJ-ez) an amount of money that a worker is paid based on the time worked

Index

balance, 4, 5, 18, 22, 23, 24, 30
cost of living, 23
COVID-19 pandemic, 14, 15
creating a budget, 4, 10, 20, 22, 30
credit cards, 24, 26
debt, 22, 24, 25, 26
debt-to-income ratio, 24, 25
deficit, 14, 15, 16
expense, 30
expenses, 4, 5, 6, 20, 22, 28, 29, 30

income, 4, 5, 6, 10, 18, 20, 22, 24, 25, 28, 30
rainy day funds, 16, 17
savings, 5, 16, 18, 20, 22, 29, 30
surplus, 14, 16
taxes, 6, 10
U.S. federal government, 6, 10, 11, 12, 13, 15, 16
U.S. state government, 6, 16, 17
wages, 4, 6, 7, 28
wants vs. needs, 4, 6, 18, 19, 20, 21, 22